How it feels

poetry written by

Dedicated to A&M

———

For the words that are so
hard to find, but we instantly
recognize when they magically
give voice to How It Feels.

CONTENTS

CHAPTER 1
Catching the Updraft

You are remarkable because
you don't love often, but
when you do, it is with depth
of heart and soul. Few things
are as bold as you.

Hang on to those who
never seek to change your
light, but rather just long
to feel it.

JmStorm

You don't need someone
to love you and solve your
problems. That does not grow
you. You need someone who
loves you and helps you see
the problems clearly, so you
can solve them yourself.

She had a way of pulling
herself back together and
becoming something that
was unstoppable.

When you're ready, I hope
you find something deep.
Something beautiful and
reliant. Something that finally
bridges the gap and connects
the dream with reality.

It is not enough to dream,
you must act. Without
action, a door is just a wall.

Be steady. Be a rock. Be the
person you want to have
around when everything has
went to hell.

I've always been fascinated at
the ability of writers to create
something out of nothing. And it's
funny how an idea can end up miles
away from what you thought. That
is the power of nothing. No chains.
Free to be anything. That is what
I think when I hear someone say,
they are nothing. I smile and say,
then you're free to be anything.

I look at you and I see a rainy
day girl who never received
the love she deserved because
it always felt conditional on
her staying in the sun.

You deserve to be loved and
to be missed. You deserve to
have someone who notices
the emptiness in the air when
you're not around.

You may not understand this
now but there are people
who need to cross your path.
They need your wisdom or
love or maybe all they need is
the feel that your soul brings
to the world.

There will be times where
you have to walk alone and it
will be completely necessary.
It will be necessary because
you are going to a place that
only you can find.

I don't hope you get the
opportunity to get even.
I hope you reach a place
where it no longer matters.

Don't be afraid to be
someone that they don't
know how to handle.

One day you will meet someone
and it will change the way you
see the world. You will be kinder.
Gentler and without realizing
it, acting out of love. And the
miracle in this is that person
didn't force the change upon you.
It was in you all along and they
brought it to the surface.

Sometimes you don't know
the answers, but you know
the feeling. And sometimes,
that is all you need.

Don't let them treat you like leftovers. Putting you in the refrigerator and pulling you out when there's nothing else to consume.

How it Feels

We are always changing and
evolving into what we wanted
to be, or what we swore we
would never become.

He did not walk away, no matter
how much she stumbled in her
darkness. He knew he couldn't
change it and he never tried. But
he stayed. He knew it was worse
to feel it all alone. Sometimes
just being there provides the
smallest rays of hope when they
have exhausted their own. And
sometimes that insignificant sliver
of light, changes everything.

Sometimes we scream because
we've been quiet for too long.
And sometimes we dance
because we've grown too still.
And sometimes we fall in love
because we open up a heart
that's been closed for too long.

Sometimes reality hurts. But
not as much as the illusion
we create when we don't
want to accept it.

How it Feels

I'm not sure I'll ever find what
I truly want. The only thing
I am sure of is that I won't
accept something that is not.

One of the things I love most
about you is the way you help me
grow. You aren't afraid to call me
out when I'm in the wrong. I didn't
know that I wanted that. I had
no idea that I needed that. But I
learned because of you that one
of the greatest demonstrations
of love is for one to facilitate
anothers growth.

Light has a way of finding
those who seek it. Just as
love has a way of healing
those who don't know
they need it.

So much of the time, what
you know isn't as crucial as
when you're willing to admit
what you don't know. That's
where the growth begins.

I hope you understand yourself
a little better this year. Because
that's the way we change. That's
the way we grow. By being able
to step outside and observe
ourselves. The maze will never
make sense as long as you look
at it like a mouse.

You may think that not saying
what you really feel is being the
bigger person by keeping the
peace, but you are wrong. You
are trading an external conflict
for an internal one. And one
day it will catch up with you.
Say what you feel.

Strength is buried in the
depths of you and the
only way you'll begin to
understand it is when you're
forced to dig for it.

Of course she had to keep
going. What choice did she
have? Her story was one that
needed to be heard and her
story wasn't finished.

You have no idea how your
words can change a life. You
really don't. They can heal
wounds. Feed the soul or be
the polaris for one who is lost
in a sea of darkness.

Sometimes we are destined for
something great. Something
beyond what we can understand
at the moment. Something past
our own imagination. So the
relationships we encounter along
the way cannot last. They are not
our destination. And so we walk
on and maybe begin to feel cursed
when in reality we just haven't
arrived where we belong.

What you have to understand is
that with knowledge also comes
patience. The more you realize
what real love is, the longer
you're willing to wait for it.

And he listened to her
intently, intrigued by her
stories of fear, strength and
grace. About being lost at
sea and finding one's heart
in the middle of a storm.

The more you understand
your own madness, the more
you realize it will never be
widely understood. Only a
few will truly get you and you
will be ok with that.

Once you become aware of
your need for growth, you
change. You can recognize the
people and relationships that
allow that growth. And more
importantly, the ones that don't.

You'll know you've grown
when your instinct is to
accept an answer rather
than to change it.

You're going to fall in love and
you're going to lose your heart.
It's part of being human. It's
part of being alive. So I wouldn't
worry about the how or the
when of it all if I were you.
These things work in their own
time. The universe knows these
things. Just as every night the
stars know where they belong.

We all want the same things
in someone. We want passion.
We want to be loved. We want
to be understood. But we also
want the security in someone
that allows us to cross lines that
we never thought we would.

So many see her beauty only
in her destination. Only in what
she's become. But they miss
so much in doing so. Because
the truth is the beauty is in her
journey. And the beauty in that
is her journey never ends.

The thing you've got to wrap
your head around is there are
so many who measure love in
proportion to the amount of
pain that comes with it. They are
conditioned to toxicity. And it
doesn't matter who loves them
the way they deserve, until they
realize this, they will repeat the
pattern again and again.

I know you hurt sometimes. But
that is because you cross lines.
You push boundaries. You take
risks and you won't be satisfied
by taking the word of others.
You have to go there for yourself
and see it. You have to feel it.
And all those things are bound to
hurt you sometimes. But that is
one of the things that make you,
beautifully you.

How it Feels

In the end it comes down
to the moments of beautiful
honesty with yourself. Moments
that you didn't give a damn
what everyone else thought.

What you think of me
means nothing. You have no
understanding of my scars, and
even less of how I got them.

She's in a tough place that
she never wanted to be. But
she remembers how far she's
traveled and that everything is
all right. It's a dot on the map.
A name of a small town she's
passing through on a road that is
taking her to where she belongs.
A place where she is free.

Some hellos are special.
Extraordinary. They are
soothing and in some not fully
understood way, they make
the world feel right. Like an
overdue love letter lost in the
mail, finally delivered.

How it Feels

She stood before the storm
without fear. But instead
feeling a kinship with the
chaos and fury.

If it should ever come down
to the choice of being loved
or growing, I hope you choose
growth. Real love won't require
you to remain static.

The truth is, you can change your
life. But you can't think of it that
way. One. Pick one thing that you
will work on conquering. Make
it a reachable goal. And when
you reach it, make another that
is within reach. Success builds
on itself. Soon, you'll want to do
more. You'll want to fix more. And
then it will hit you. The hardest
part is learning a new mindset.

I hope you have the courage to
let it be what it will be. Allow
it to fall apart if it must. To be
brave enough to believe your
happiness is possible in a life
you had never considered.

She hasn't given up on love,
but she is seeing things for
what they are. She is not going
to waste her time on a man
who values her fruit but doesn't
understand her shade.

I understand that it's hard to know which way to go. The truth is that life can get so loud sometimes. Everywhere you turn you are being influenced on what to buy. What to think. What to be. But once you become aware of that, you begin to hear yourself from all the noise.

CHAPTER 2
Making Sense of the Noise

Sometimes people don't want
answers. They're not ready for
them. Sometimes all they really
need in that moment is to know
that someone else has been
there too.

One day you will find
someone who gets it. They
will crave the understanding
of you, Because they crave
the depth that follows it.

You're going to go through some
hard times. They are a part of life,
but they will build you. You'll have
some sunny days along the way,
just as you should. They keep you
believing. But they won't shape
you like the wind does. They won't
build courage like the lightning or
cleanse your soul like the rain.

She was never going to be
someone he would risk it all for,
and he would never know the
respect that she longed to have for
her man. Long story short, they
didn't belong together and I think
they both knew it. It was a house
of cards that went up quickly. They
knew to not question the flimsy
floor or the shaky walls. But they
didn't really know each other at all.

Some day you'll look back at all
this and you'll realize that it wasn't
a series of mistakes. One day
you'll love yourself a little deeper,
if for no other reason than the
way your heart made it through.

Masculinity isn't toxic. Being
a man isn't toxic. Being a
selfish and controlling child,
in a man's body, is.

Feeling things deeply seems like a curse at first. But that's because you don't understand it all. I've been there and I know. It's just random noise. But once you begin to comprehend that what you feel has meaning and purpose and that nothing is random, everything changes. You begin to understand people and yourself and just how you fit into all this madness.

You are good enough. Only you
can set that standard. But realize
that you may have to walk alone
for a bit. Because not everyone will
recognize it. We all see the night
sky, but only a few of us actually
see the stars.

I know how it feels. To live
in a world that falls for the
look while you always fall
for the feel.

It's interesting how we recognize
someone much like ourselves,
like an unspoken code that you
just pick up on. Even though
you've much to learn about them,
you are aware that you're on
the same frequency and feel the
world in a similar way.

Truth can be either a slap to
the face or a kiss on the lips.
Many times it comes down to
how we choose to embrace it.

Sometimes you'll spend
a lifetime untangling the
knots that you did not tie.

Appearances are deceiving.
We are all a fucking mess
on the inside. Even the best
looking suit is held together
with stitches.

How it Feels

Sometimes we are tired
because we are too unaware
of how much energy we spend,
trying to hold together that
which is meant to come apart.

Take care of your people.
Be it blood or soul related.
Have their back and give
them your shoulder.

Sometimes people just want
to know that they are needed.
That they have a purpose in
your life and by being in it, they
make it a little bit better.

Always remember; people
won't try to destroy that
which they love. People try
to destroy possessions they
no longer own.

Numbness has a way of sinking
in without you even realizing it.
Communicating just becomes a
way of exchanging information.
And you don't realize how
numb you've become until you
connect with someone who
makes you feel.

Some people want security
while others want to feel
things that those people will
never understand.

How it Feels

And eventually you realize
that real love comes down
to feeling safe enough to
be vulnerable.

I don't know what to tell you.
You have to give people a
chance and at the same time you
have to be smart and look out
for yourself.That is the finest line
you can walk. Because so many
fall to one side or the other.

If you want to understand her
then you have to realize that
everything she says is relevant.
But you cannot think about it in
terms of the way you interpret
things. You must think about
why it is significant to her.

You say that you want to take
care of her, and I'm sure that's
true. But you have to understand
that it requires more than mere
physical action. Take care of her
emotionally and mentally. Listen
to her. Let her pour her heart out
on you. Show her exactly what a
rock is made of.

Understand she will have moments
where she's hesitant, even resistant
to allowing herself to lean on you.
And that goes back to trust. Not
just of you, but the trust in herself.
She's made mistakes and believed
those who she shouldn't have.
But in hindsight, she should have
recognized it. It takes time because
trusting yourself again involves a
little self given grace.

And the truth is that you
never really get over deep
love. You will carry it for the
rest of your life. You only get
over your expectations.

And so many people are ready
to move on to whatever life
has next. The next love. The
next rush. The next next. That
explains so much about our
world. So many are in a never
ending search for something
that makes them feel complete.

Lots of people love flowers.
Some cut them while others
plant them. Remember that.

If you don't know me, it might
seem that I don't care. But that
isn't the case. It's just that I've
had to learn how to control it.
Because when I allow it, I care
too much.

She seems cold to those
who rationalized her fire and
neglected to feel it.

Something sacred. That was the
conclusion she came to and she didn't
come there easily. The truth is she
had known love at the extremes. She
was tired of hands that could so easily
tear down what they had built, as if it
meant nothing. She had grown weary
of a tongue that poisoned every sweet
word shared before because a moment
of rage for what god only knows.
Something sacred. That was clear
to her. A man who viewed the bond
between them as something worth
defending. A good man who holds a
few things up to be holy.

I disconnected from the idea
that I had to have someone,
just to have someone. As if to
save me from myself. I need
synchronicity. I required the
communion of understanding. I
wanted the resonance of truth
and the cohesion of trust.

Some will tell you when you're
wrong just to put you in your
place. And someone who loves
you can do the same and it feels
completely different. They tell
you because they love you and
they don't want you to be wrong.
Love changes everything.

She will give up her coat and
shiver to warm another. She will
quietly take care of things so
it doesn't weigh others down.
She is selfless to a fault. And
she does it without asking for
anything. Not even recognition.
but she can't help but wonder if
anyone wonders if she's ok. and
that is the tragedy. A beautiful
soul who is left to ponder if she
even matters.

People will drift in and out of
your life and the best advice
I can give you is to honor
the current.

To truly understand you, you
must understand the reasons
behind what you do. Nothing
is random, our actions
have history.

How it Feels

At some point you begin
to realize that love means
investment. They'll invest their
time. Their emotions. Their mind
and their heart. Not for what they
can get out of it, but because
they believe you are worthy of it.

She seemed hard to please for
many, but she really wasn't. She
just knew what she wanted and
when you know that, you know
what you don't want. The same
energy and loyalty. That's it. It
was all she ever wanted.

How it Feels

She's ok now and she knows it.
But sometimes she questions it
because she has never really let
her guard down. That's what she
fears most. Being unprepared
due to a false sense of security.

She makes complete sense to
me because she doesn't get
attached to things. She falls in
love with moments that speak
to her soul.

You shouldn't have to convince
others into loyalty no more than
you should convince them to be
truthful. They either have it or
they don't and it is not your job
to change it.

Sometimes we try to force a
new beginning when all we really
need is a few moments of clarity.
Because that's a gift, being able
to see things clearly. And when it
comes to figuring out where you
are going, it's a must.

She will test you and see what
you're made of, just by being
herself. Because the nature of a
strong woman will identify who a
man really is. If he feels threatened
or has the need to possessively
control her, it will be revealed. And
the funny thing is that she doesn't
want to call the shots. She wants a
man who will embrace her strength
and stand by her side. A man who
will walk with her but will lead with
taking the first step.

Before you go any further with her, you should know that she is unforgettable. And if you don't give her your attention in her presence, she will undoubtedly claim it with her absence.

How it Feels

You seeing her as beautiful and
her feeling it about herself are
two completely separate things.

You learn to appreciate the
moment once you realize that
the moment will always end.

Some are just different. They
need the light that the sun
brings, but long to connect with
the soul of the storm.

She has an amazing capacity to care and her love is strong. And yet she remains alone. Because her heart is guarded and her intuition is never wrong.

One thing I've learned in this life
is that we plant the seeds of our
unhappiness the more we try to
hang on. Because this life is so much
of learning how to let go. Eventually
we'll have to let it all go because it
all ends. People move on and pass
on. Situations change, so do people
and one day we'll have to let it go.
And sometimes the hardest one to
turn loose is the notion in our head
of how it's all supposed to be.

You've not really felt beauty until
you've seen her without the mask.
Not until you've seen the lace of
the intimate things she holds deep
inside do you begin to understand
the scars. The damage and the
pain she has trouble finding
the words to describe. She's an
unconventional story and one that
is so often misunderstood because
some of her beauty can only be
found in the dark.

How it Feels

It takes a strong man, secure
in himself to embrace a strong
woman. Only the weak who
feels threatened would try to
extinguish that kind of fire.

I'd rather you not ask me a question if you are unwilling to accept my answer. I'm not saying you must agree with it, but respect it enough that you don't feel compelled to manipulate me into changing it.

And some seem to stay
disconnected. As if they cannot
fall. But the truth is they know
when they do, they will not be able
to stop it. They love too much and
give all they have, and through it
all, they know that's how it should
be. They've just done it too many
times for the wrong soul.

CHAPTER 3
Words of the Heart

Of course I noticed your beautiful
skin and the art it created that
spoke to my carnal mind. But that
was a conversation with my lust. It
was your elegant heart that spoke
to my depths and that kind of
exchange never really goes away.
Its words burned into my soul.

You are more beautiful than
you know. And that in itself,
is beautiful.

Sometimes it becomes too much
and her patience has wore too
thin. That is when you have to
step in on her behalf. Giving her a
morning that is focused on her. Her
tea in bed. Stirring her laughter.
Inviting her pleasure. Life becomes
overwhelming and that is best
fought with overwhelming love.

To really understand her, you must
go beyond the words and grasp
the reasons of her actions. So if
she asks a lot of questions, realize
she wants to learn your world.
And if she hugs you for no reason,
know she wants you to feel loved.

The truth is I didn't want to want
you. I didn't want to lose control
of my thoughts. I didn't want
to feel the void of need. Just
understand you are a well fought
secret obsession. A war of attrition
that I would never be able to win.

I know you. In a world of billions
and all that we learn through
life, I know you. I learned, you.
There's something incredibly
beautiful about that.

All I know is that I love you.
Bone deep and the duration
of souls.

Touching you left a
piece of infinity in me. A
fragment of unforgettable.
A sliver of forever.

How it Feels

And when I finally found her,
she asked me where I had
been all this time. I got lost,
I said, and I ended up taking
the long way home.

Nothing makes you feel
as unique and as loved as
another seeing you for who
you really are. Someone
who looks into your soul and
cannot look away.

Underneath every I love you
that we share is silence. And
beneath that silence is our
truth that need not be said,
but is impossible to not feel.

When we connect, it is so much
more than that. It's deeper. We
collide. But it's not a violent event
because there is no resistance. It's
like I feel you freely mixing with me.
In the mind and through the rest of
me. Your words. Your thoughts and
the person i've always known you
to be, it all combines with me. And
when that happens, it is impossible
for me to feel separate from you.
Impossible to feel alone.

I think we connect because I know
the battles you've fought and
the wars you've waged that you
never wanted. That's what binds
some. It's not the things they own
or the position they hold, but the
struggles they've known.

I hope you know that I love you.
But more than that, I hope you
understand that when I say I love
you, it means that I see a part of
you in me. It means I accept you
and invest in you, just as you are.

It was like you could see inside
me and you saw that I had so
much love to give in this life when
I thought I had nothing left. It was
insightful and it was endearing.
And it was but one of the many
things that stole my heart.

I need you and the life that you
bring. You brought fire to cold
ash. Flow to stagnation. You
rescued me from a slow death of
the contentment of standing still.
You are the medicine I needed
when I didn't realize I was ill.

I've seen under your hard
shell and experienced what
few ever have. I've kissed the
wounded parts. I've heard the
tremble of tender words and
I've beheld the beauty of a
soul that feels so much.

And if you want her to feel
special, then you have to treat
her special. It is as simple as that.
Anything less and she'll know
it's a fraud. You can't speak of
diamonds and give her broken
glass to walk on.

When you find beautiful depth
with someone, nothing else will
ever do. Nothing else will ever be
good enough. Because you have
been awakened to the fact that
mere moments in the abyss holds
more intimacy than years on the
surface. And once you become
conscious to that, there is no
going back to sleep.

And if you settle, don't settle for just
love. Because there's no shortage
of those who'll love you today, but
become distant when things get tough.
And you can count on that things will
get tough. It will never be smooth
sailing with the love of your life, all the
way to the end. You need someone
who'll love you to the end. Someone
who'll be there through the thick and
thin of things. Someone whose love
is absolute. Someone who's made
the decision that nothing will come
between you and them.

She ached to be held when the moon was high and the tide was closing in. To be touched, kissed and fondled by his hands. She longed to feel him not just on the surface, but deeper. Below the mantle and closer to the core.

You bring a certain softness to
the morning, an elegance to the
sheets that cannot be explained
in any other way than it is good
for my soul.

Some days I just need you. I need
the light, the energy and to feel
the depth that has always existed
between us. I get too dark and a
little too shallow from this world
and I simply need you.

We hold close the ones
who found the way in. And
even closer to the one who
understood what they saw.

I had a feeling about you. Like there was something worth knowing. Something worth understanding. And although I didn't know it at the time, it was something worth loving.

I don't want to fight you, nor
surrender. I want something
beautifully in the middle where
there is flow. A place where we
balance each other, compliment
each other and we become
stronger together.

They will never fully
understand our nuances. Our
give and take. Our ebb and
flow. They try to comprehend
the waves between us without
realizing it has a lot to do with
the moon an the ocean that
has always been you and me.

She'll have days when she'll
just cry. Like clouds that have
become too heavy and the
rain has to fall. Don't be that
guy who makes her feel like it's
something she can't openly do.
Be that guy who loves her. Who
stays close, holds her tight and
isn't afraid of getting wet.

She got quiet when she stopped to
re-examine her path that had become
so difficult. Shutting out the world
and finding a sense of direction by
taking in her surroundings. It was so
different from what she had imagined
10 years ago. Finding her bearings
from the things she knew to be true
was crucial because in order to know
where you are going, you must first
establish where you are.

There are moments when she
needs your touch more than
your words. Moments that are
void of advice and solutions. Just
hold her in the silence and let
what she's feeling flow into you.
Embrace it. Feel it. Believe it or
not, that's communication. That's
an empathy she can relate to. A
form of care she can feel.

Be easy on your heart and
take it slow when healing. It
has experienced things you
have yet to understand.

The holidays aren't the same
for everyone. For some, it's a
day to awkwardly sit down next
to the void they've avoided all
year. A day to shake hands with
the pain they've worked around
for so long.

You are not perfect, we all have
our flaws. But you have a grace
that is intoxicating to me.

My hope for the new year
is that it finds these arms
having realized their purpose.
Wrapped around you, like they
were always meant to be.

What she loved about him
was the balance he provided.
He was a good man with a
good heart that understood
when to pull her hair.

It's a scene that has played
many times in my mind.
Witnessing your comfort with
being vulnerable. To me. Not
needing it, but desiring it.
Watching you fall in love with
your unguarded freedom.

I am part of you, which is to say
I have to be inside you in some
way. A fire in your heart. A swirl in
your mind. An occupation under
your skin. There is a part of me
that is yours and will never be
content on the outside.

I don't know how you did it, but
you just walked right into my
soul. As if it was something you
had done many times before.

I don't know what all this means,
but I know what it means to me.
You make me feel, intensely. It is
something that is raw and organic,
like a captivating book that no one
has ever picked up. That's a rare
thing in today's rehashed world.
And for that, I read on.

It's always been the connection
with you. Even when we didn't
talk, it was there. It would always
be there. Some people will
leave you words you will always
remember and others will leave
a feel your soul cannot forget.

She embraced his hands and
welcomed the vulnerability they
forced upon her. With so many
decisions to be made in her
day to day, it felt good to be
relieved of any choice.

I'll never forget you. How could I? You unapologetically made me feel more than I could have ever thought possible. And for that. I will always love you.

The real you. That's all I want and all I'll ever ask. I know you learned to suppress your beautiful heart because the deaf and numb made you feel that it was necessary. But I am not one of them. Don't silence your heart with me because it says so much that I understand.

So many people don't even know
what they want to do with their lives,
but I am one of the fortunate ones. I
want to spend my days taking care of
you. Cooking you savory meals and
learning how to make your tea. I want
to draw your bath and wash your hair
and I want to write about all of it, the
beautiful work I have found.

You and me. I love how those
words have the power to change
the way I think. Like new evidence
that overthrows old verdicts.

There's something beautiful about baring your soul, including the parts you may perceive to be ugly to another human. All the while aware of the fear that they may turn away from it. But they don't. Instead they love you deeper for it.

And one of the things that I adore
about you is the elegant purity of
your face. It is a timeless beauty
that I would recognize in any part
of the world. A conversation with
my eyes that I would understand
in any lifetime.

It's that feeling of belonging. That
sense of where I am supposed to
be. With you. And when I am away,
it only magnifies it and I am left
with three beautifully sad words.
I miss you. I miss you because so
much of you feels like home.

In a world full of so many actors,
I love how you know who you
are. Sometimes bandaging
the wounded and sometimes
swinging the sword, but always
real. Always led by the heart.

You are my weakness. The thing
is I lack the power to say no to.
Whether it was loving you when
you were near, or feeding your
memory after you were gone. It
just wasn't in me to do nothing
and let you slip away.

She is a wilderness that you
cannot learn in a day. You
must become lost in her and
go a little mad.

You can get lost in her eyes.
Learn every beautiful curve.
But until you know her heart,
you know nothing.

There is a rawness about her
that many don't understand.
She is chaos in the wind and
fire across the sky and not
everyone can appreciate the
beauty of a storm.

That's the part about us that
always gets me. The balance. The
balance of how it feels so right
and it makes so much sense. It is
the blending of the feel with the
beautiful logic of it all.

How it Feels

I like to think that we were
supposed to meet. I like to
think that I needed the color
that you added to my life.

Understand that I never tire of
listening to you. It doesn't matter
if it's something spectacular or just
the account of a terrible day. Just
know it matters to me because
you matter to me. When we talk,
I feel you. And that is something I
never grow tired of.

How it Feels

And the truth is you have
always been the only one in
the room for me. The whisper
that sounds like a conscience I
cannot ignore.

I am amazed by your ability to always find the soft parts in me. Without even knowing, you run your fingers through the sweet soil in my soul. The place where beautiful things grow.

I watch you as you pull off your
shirt and pay the attention your
body demands. Beautiful flowing
lines and the blessing of your
curves. Uninterrupted by color
and cloth. Free of fabric that
was designed to mold you into
a civilized state. A river as it was
always meant to be seen. Free.

Through it all I always believed I
would be ok. Like I knew it would
all work out because I always
believed in the someday where I
would meet someone like you.

How it Feels

I am lost in you and lost in the
beautiful wilderness that lie
between loving you and wanting
you. Somewhere between aching
to touch your skin and needing
to feel your soul.

He had a feel about him that
she hadn't really known before.
It was that warm feeling of
comprehension. The comfort of
feeling understood. Almost as if
he opened her heart and read its
pages to her. And for the first time,
it made complete sense to her.

How it Feels

I like to think I was always meant
to feel you. To learn the stories of
your heart and how it kept itself
intact. Like I was destined to feel
the waves sent out from the impact
of your presence in this life.

You're an old soul. And I think that's one of the things that I connect with the most. Like a wanton kiss that hangs in the air like an autumn moon. A two am sleepless thought. A folded love letter that one hangs onto for life.

And your voice isn't just any
voice. It's special. It's the calm
that washes over me like a
warm summer rain. It's the light
that scatters the darkness like a
sunrise. It's the once numb heart
that feels so deeply again.

You leave me breathless and a
little broken inside from feeling
the void created by the distance
between us. Treading water in
this sea of desire and dreaming
of your land. Longing to crawl
upon your shore.

CHAPTER 4
Caring for the Wound

I don't know the story of your
pain or the number of days that
you've carried it around, but I
do know it changed the way
you see yourself. And that is a
tragedy that no one hears about.
A beautiful soul that had to learn
to live with a wounded heart.

The soul has moments when it
can only understand the rain.

One day we will connect again
and it will feel as though we
never parted. One day we will
cry for what time took from us,
and laugh at what it couldn't.

Change is so difficult because of the unknown. And sometimes, in our mind at least, the known bad is better than all the unanswerable questions. It's why we stay in bad relationships and at bad jobs. It's easier to keep doing what you've been doing. We rationalize out all the bad and pretty soon there isn't much of a compelling case for the unknown.

I thought I knew you, but looking
back I realize that all I really knew
was the combination of what you
and I wanted me to believe.

Your healing has to be more
important than your fragile ego.
Moving on to someone else
without having healed is a self
serving illusion.

As you get older you begin to realize that you are made up of so many broken things. Things you believed could certainly destroy you but instead shattered against you. The pieces become part of you, like little shards of broken glass that sometimes hurt, but could never break you.

Eventually I had to let go. But no matter where I go from here, you will always be the reason I pause. The memory that will not fade. The small pocket of silence in a world full of noise.

Give it time. Life has a way of
showing you what you need to see
when you are able to understand it,
touching the parts that need to feel
and making whole the places you
thought would never heal.

The reason it hurts to lose
some is because they made
a place in your heart. A place
that is just theirs and can
never be filled again.

I think when you love someone, really love someone, part of that never fades away. Even when you've grown and no longer want to be with them, part of them lingers. Part of them will always remain in the depths of the ocean that is your soul.

Through it all, I've always
believed that you would find
me again. If not in this life, then
in the next. Water always finds
its way back to the sea and we
were an ocean.

I know it's hard walking in a
downpour and sometimes it
feels like the rain won't end. But
one day you will notice it has
stopped and you will also notice
what it washed away.

We may not be able to control
how we feel, but we can
understand why we feel the way
we do. And that is such a huge
step in healing. Understanding
what rips open old wounds.

Sometimes that's all you need.
Someone who gets it. A little
light in the darkness. Some
empathy in a cold world. A little
understanding of the chaos inside.

What they don't tell you is that
sometimes it's not over, when it's
over. And it never will be. Like a
book with the last chapter torn
out. And you are left to wonder
what is on the missing pages. The
lack of closure can be tough on the
soul, writing out the final words to
a book with ink that can never dry.

I hope you find the love that
still sees your beauty when you
are a mess, your light when you
have become dark and your path
when you are lost.

Sometimes we don't walk away
from people who aren't good for
us because of our own guilt. As
if walking away proves we don't
love them. But as any addict who
has come clean can tell you, it
proves you still love yourself.

I hate that you had to go through
it, but I also feel sorry for those
who took your heart for granted.
They could see and yet were
blind. Able to touch, but too numb
to feel. Of sound mind, but could
not understand.

How it Feels

Sometimes it's not the what
went wrong that bothers you.
Sometimes what bothers you
the most is that it never was
right and for time, you didn't
know the difference.

Sometimes we don't want to
heal because the pain is the
last link to what we've lost.

Sometimes we cause our own
pain. Unaware we have become
stuck in a single chapter because
we will not write off those that
don't belong in our story.

She's not broken, she just doesn't
know what to do. When she loves,
she's all in. following her heart
is just her way. But that kind of
vulnerability can hurt deep when it's
met with betrayal. How do I come
back from that? She asks herself.
How do I trust my own judgement
when the last time I followed my
heart, it led me to a place so foreign
and far from where I belong? That's
the problem. She's not broken. She
just doesn't have an answer.

I know she has dark spots
inside of her, but don't we all?
It's knowing them and their
history that makes her real.
Human. Flawed, beautifully so.

Don't deny what you feel. To do
so won't make it go away, but
only buries it. And buried things
sometimes make us react without
thinking. Acknowledge it. Dig down
to the roots in order to understand
it. That's where the power is. You
can feel things deeply and still keep
your shit together.

You can't hold yourself back, waiting for an apology. Because it's an acknowledgement of, at least for a moment, who we are. And the truth is some can never come to terms with that. Not to you and not to themselves.

I cannot heal you. But I can love
you in your darkness. Hold your
hand while you process the pain.
I can be the silk in your hands as
you close the wound.

Just keep working and making
your life better. Mentally.
Emotionally. And realize you're
going to lose people along the
way because they no longer fit
with that goal.

Don't be discouraged by the bad
things that happen. There is balance
in these things. Because there is no
sense of accomplishment without
some struggle. And sometimes you
don't recognize what is real until you
learn to identify what is fake.

How it Feels

And the pain became too
overwhelming. So I got busy.
Fixing this and creating that.
I filled my time with things I
could control. For some, it is the
alchemy of turning an ache of
the heart into a memory.

And it's not that I didn't feel anymore pain after you. It's just that your presence made it something manageable. Something that I could at any time stand above and feel the sun. That's what happens someone loves you and says, I'm not going to let you feel it alone.

You can do all the work, all the
things to help you heal, and you
will still have moments that stop
you in your tracks. A memory that
will make you question the distance
between you and your injury. It's
ok. It happens. You're not the same
person with the same perspective.
You are a human vessel, carrying
memories of the past.

I get it. It hurts too much to think about. So we put it off. We deny our grief. But in doing so, we deny our healing. There's no way around that because the truth is there is information in our grief. Not just what someone meant to us, but buried underneath it all, a glimpse to who we really are.

Maybe there is a lesson buried
in the hurt. A little order to be
found in the chaos of our hearts.
We give too many chances to
those who don't deserve them
and use the evidence against
someone new.

There is a healing property in
your touch. A mending quality
that I cannot explain. But I know
it is there and I feel it down deep
where there are wounds that no
one sees.

I cannot stop your spiral, but I can
wrap my arms around you until
it begins to make sense. I cannot
drown out the voices in your
head, but I can whisper it's ok until
they fade. I am not afraid of your
darkness. I do not despise your
mess. I fear your inability to see
what I see. A beautiful soul.

I am fine, but also none of
your concern. And I am certain
that at least one of those is
completely true.

How it Feels

The things we miss the most are
often the things that touched us
the most. The things that found
their way in and made their
home some place deep.

I know it's hard to turn your back and walk away. Even when they don't seem to care about the pain they inflict. You've put a lot of heart and soul into them and that is not something you can suddenly pretend never happened. It meant something. And even as you take the first steps, it still does.

Sometimes you just need space
to yourself. Time to reflect and
heal in the silence. A need to
lower the sails and drift for a
while. Lost in the sea and your
own madness.

Sporadic attention is not interest. It is manipulative and only serves to keep you from moving on.

Some have known too much
hurt and have metabolised
too much pain. And so that is
all they have to give. They are
poisoned by it, not realizing
that even their fruit is bitter.

Sometimes I think of you and
where you might be. I hope
you're happy. I hope you're
well. And above all, I hope
you feel free.

And when you look back, I hope you don't dwell on the mistakes. We've all made those. No, I hope you see metal that was tempered by a life that was lived.

We begin to let go the
moment we realize our best
will never be good enough.

And if they have broken you,
you must know that you can
never go back. I don't care how
much you love them or how
much you think this time will be
different. The fact is they didn't
care enough to keep you intact.

One day it will all make sense.
One day you will realize that
those who couldn't or wouldn't
stay are just a reminder of what
you at one time thought you
wanted, before you learned the
worth of your heart.

Sometimes falling apart is the way
we shake loose the pieces that
just don't belong anymore. It's as
natural as the wind and rain. So
cry if you need to. Scream if you
must. But never lose sight of what
it really is. A thunderstorm that
clears the air.

One of the hardest things to
mend is one's own broken heart.
Purging beautiful things from
it after the realization that they
only mattered to you.

And one of the most beautiful
paradoxes goes something like
this; you don't know how it ends,
and yet somehow you know it
doesn't end like this.

Forgiveness is grace and
grace isn't demanded.

There's a certain beautiful
intimacy that comes with learning
someone's pain. A nearness that
few will experience. A closeness
that many will never grasp.

One of the saddest things is
the realization that there are
many beautiful hearts hidden
away. Judged by the owner to
be unseemly because of the
scars it bears.

You shouldn't have to over think it. It shouldn't be necessary to pore over their words, trying to find their true meaning. The truth is, the language of pure love is simple and easy to understand.

I'm not going to tell you it's all going to be ok. That's the easy thing to do and then drift away. You deserve better than that. I don't know how it'll work out, but I will hang around to make sure you are ok.

Looking back, I still don't know what to say about us. The words aren't as accurate as I would like and maybe that's because I'm still processing what it meant. It was like witnessing an eclipse that's come and gone. It was otherworldly. It was magical. And years later you cannot forget that for a few moments, the land was void of any shadows.

You know that you're in a better place when you can acknowledge the good times without any need to tear them down. You've reached a place of honesty. Good things sometimes end. That's part of healing and part of letting go.

Where to Follow JmStorm

———

Facebook: facebook.com/Jmstormquotes

Tumblr: jmstormquotes.tumblr.com

Instagram: @jmstormquotes

X: @storm_jon